www.ingramcontent.com/pod-product-compliance
Lightning Source LLC
Chambersburg PA
CBHW051635160426
43209CB00004B/652

Beneath the Surface of Soil

Under the ground, where chaos reigns,
Earthworms crack jokes, avoiding the rains.
Microbes gossip, all in a fuss,
While roots play tag, no need to rush.

The underground party is full of cheer,
Silly fungi draw friends near.
With toadstools spinning tales so grand,
Life thrives in the dark, a merry band.

Little critters munch on a treat,
As carrots and beets tap their feet.
They wink at the radishes, all red and round,
In this secret realm, laughter is found.

So when you dig, give a shout,
For beneath the soil, there's fun about.
Every root whispers, every seed beams,
Nature's soil is full of dreams!

Signs and Symbols in the Saplings

Little saplings stretch and yawn,
Sharing giggles at the break of dawn.
Symbols woven with twig and leaf,
A sign of nature's silly belief.

One sprout wears glasses quite askew,
While another shouts, "I see you!"
In wind's embrace, they sway and sway,
Gossiping stories, come what may.

Old branches peek, rolling their eyes,
At the antics, beneath the skies.
Everything's funny in this leafy nook,
As saplings share their carefree book.

So let's write tales, let joy take flight,
Among the signs that feel just right.
Every tree's secret gives us the scoop,
Nature's hieroglyphs, hilarious group!

The Poetry of Petals

Petals whisper soft and low,
With silly tales they love to show.
Daisies compete in a bloom-off fight,
Who can flash colors, oh so bright?

The tulips tease with their fancy hats,
While bees chuckle at sleepy cats.
A butterfly flits, spreading cheer,
Sipping nectar, whispering near.

Lilies laugh at the pond's slick boys,
Twirling about, having their joys.
Each flower shares an outlandish tale,
In this garden, fun shall prevail!

So skip through petals, listen well,
Every blossom has a joke to tell.
With laughter stitched in every hue,
The poetry of petals is surely true!

Whispering Roots

In a garden where secrets hide,
Roots giggle as they curl and slide.
Worms wear hats in a soil parade,
While dandelions scheme in the shade.

Frogs laugh out loud, jumping around,
As beetles dance, making a sound.
The sun winks bright, full of glee,
Nature's jesters, wild and free.

A rhubarb grins, such a sight,
As tomato plants plot with delight.
Every sprout tells a joke or two,
In this leafy world, we all knew.

So when you stroll through this green clime,
Remember, it's all just a rhyme.
For every slip, a giggling spruit,
Is life's grand comedy, that's the root!

Subtle Threads of Life

Along the vine, a spider grins,
Spinning stories as the day begins.
"Knock, knock, who's there?" she croons with zest,
Sir Bug's in for a little jest!

The trees chuckle with branches held high,
"Look at that cloud, it's passing by!"
With whispers of wind, they gently tease,
As daisies sway, laughing in the breeze.

A misfit weed waves, "I'm on my way!"
"Hold tight!" says the breeze, "You've got this, hey!"
Unlikely friends in this colorful fray,
Life's a funny game, come what may!

So as the sun sets with a wink,
Nature shares stories that make us think.
In every thread of life that we weave,
Giggles abound; just breathe and believe!

Voice of the Unseen

In the meadow, a rustle's heard,
A chorus of critters without a word.
A grasshopper leaps with a flick and a hop,
While ants host a party; they never stop!

The ladybugs laugh, each has a tale,
Of lost socks and a bug in a gale.
A butterfly swings by, with flair so bright,
Whispering secrets in the golden light.

"Who left crumbs on the path?" they exclaim,
A mystery dance, a cheeky game.
Nature's jesters with giggles and cheer,
In this secret world, nothing's unclear.

So gather 'round as shadows play,
Join the chat where the wild things sway.
In every rustle, jesters thrive,
In the voice of the unseen, we come alive!

Ethereal Conversations

In the twilight, shadows peek,
A shy flower starts to speak.
The moon giggles, a luminous grin,
As night's antics quietly begin.

A dandelion dreams of flight,
Chasing stars through the silly night.
"Catch me if you can!" it shouts with glee,
As fireflies buzz, "Come dance with me!"

The moonbeam chuckles, slipping by,
While owls hoot jokes; oh my, oh my!
In tangled vines, the laughter grows,
Whispered fun where no one knows.

So lean in close, take a good look,
Nature's storytellers, not in a book.
In each nook, where shadows play,
Listen well, they have much to say!

The Rustling Soliloquy

In the garden, secrets fly,
Leaves giggle as they dance by.
A squirrel nods, his hat askew,
Plotting mischief, just for a view.

Breeze whispers tales of grand delight,
Of sunbaked days and cool, crisp nights.
The daisies gossip, oh what a scene,
While sleepy bees hum in between.

A clumsy bug trips on a stem,
Shrugs it off and calls it a gem.
They all laugh, there's nothing to fear,
Nature's comedy is always near.

So let's toast to the leaves so bold,
Sharing tales of shenanigans old.
In every rustle, laughter sings,
Life's little jokes, oh what joy it brings!

The Canvas of Green Dreams

Brushstrokes of green fill the air,
Laughing leaves without a care.
The canvas twirls with shades of fun,
Creating giggles 'neath the sun.

A brush of wind, the colors blend,
Dancing daisies, best of friends.
In every patch, a riot blooms,
As nature laughs in sunny rooms.

Budding Conversations

In every bud, a story waits,
Their tiny tales can twist fates.
Petals chatter, a gossip spree,
Over who's best at shady glee.

Sunflowers wink with golden rays,
Encouraging tiny sprout displays.
Each bloom joins in with vibrant cheer,
Sprouting jokes that all can hear.

Intimacy of the Understory

Beneath the ferns, a party brews,
With ladybugs, sharing their news.
Whispers float on a breeze so light,
As shadows dance in fading light.

A mushroom's cap wears a silly grin,
While ants parade their loot within.
Together they laugh, in leafy lounges,
Creating joy in nature's bounds.

Whispers on the Wind

Between the leaves, a giggle flies,
A secret shared beneath the skies.
In rustling grass, a sly jest bends,
Nature's humor, where laughter lends.

A dandelion with a flair,
Waves hello, with no real care.
Tickling toes, it jumps around,
With cheeky roots in funny ground.

Whispers of the Flora

A robin perches, a curious spy,
Hearing tales from a daisies' sly reply.
"Have you seen the grasshopper's jumpy spree?"
Laughter echoes, wild and free.

The tulips wear hats made of morning dew,
While the violets wink at the skies so blue.
A playful banter, a chuckle or two,
As petals exchange their gossip anew.

Breezes carry jokes from tree to tree,
With a swirl of leaves, oh what a spree!
The meadow erupts in a symphonic cheer,
The whispers of life, oh so dear.

So join in the fun, take a leaf and grin,
In the laughter of nature, let the joy begin.
With each rustle and hum, we find our way,
In these gentle echoes that brighten the day.

Unseen Threads of Connection

In the underbrush, where the shadows twine,
Roots whisper secrets like aged vintage wine.
A dandelion grins, with seeds like dreams,
Gentle connections through silvery beams.

The earthworms work, scrubbing the ground,
While ants parade in a fine merry round.
Mysteries woven by a spider's span,
All tied together by nature's own plan.

A poke of a flower, a nod of a leaf,
In this green web, joy hides like a thief.
Through laughter and sunshine, we find our link,
In nature's odd humor, we pause and think.

So tread light and easy where the critters play,
In the shades of the green, let worries decay.
For unseen connections always discern,
In the glorious ruckus, there's much to learn.

Songs of the Sunlit Glade

In the glade where sunbeams bounce,
Frogs croak out a joyful flounce.
A chorus of chirps from the bugs on cue,
Makes the flowers sway and the grass dance too.

The mushrooms twirl in a fungal ballet,
While a squirrel jives, trying to splay.
With acorns as maracas, oh what a sight,
Nature's own party from morning till night.

The wind plays notes through the willow's leaves,
It hummed a tune that never deceives.
Chasing butterflies that waltz on by,
In a realm where every giggle is nigh.

So gather the laughter, let it unfold,
In the sunlit embrace, the stories retold.
With each playful twitch, in this glorious space,
Life's real anthem, a whimsical race.

Veils of the Verdant

In the garden where giggles grow,
Leaves dance lightly, putting on a show.
The daisies gossip, the ferns conspire,
With a tickle of breeze, they never tire.

Laughter spreads from one sprout to the next,
A secret club where all are perplexed.
Petals flutter like whispers of cheer,
While a snail slides by, ever so near.

The clovers chuckle, playing hide and seek,
With tiny bees all buzzing a streak.
A parade of colors, a carnival sight,
Nature's jesters under sunlight bright.

Oh, the antics of roots that entwine,
They wiggle and giggle, that's truly divine.
In this playful patch, where strange things occur,
The tales of the green, oh how they stir.

The Echoing Green

In a meadow where the echoes play,
Funny voices drift and sway.
A breeze carries a joke from afar,
While daisies chime like a laughing star.

A brook bubbles, chatting along,
Frogs croak back, singing a song.
Whimsical reeds in unison sway,
Dancing to nature's own ballet.

Laughter flies with the birds on high,
Witty quips in the open sky.
The grass whispers secrets, tickles and teases,
While nature's chorus fills with breezes.

Join the echo, let your voice soar,
In this green realm, we laugh more.
Where every chuckle finds its place,
In the heart of the earth's embrace.

Conversations in the Shade

Under the boughs where shadows meet,
Grasshoppers gossip, skipping a beat.
A squirrel shares a nutty joke,
Trees laugh loudly, their leaves all stroke.

The mushrooms nod with wisdom grand,
Twirling their caps like a frothy band.
Sunbeams slip through a playful glance,
Encouraging worms to do a dance.

A cricket chirps a witty retort,
While beetles roll like they're at court.
The wise old oak leans in to hear,
Joking that roots hold secrets dear.

In this refuge from sunlight's glare,
Every critter has tales to share.
Join the frenzy, don't be late,
For laughter thrives in nature's fate.

Blooms of Reflection

In a field where odd thoughts collide,
Petals laugh while roots confide.
A tulip winks, tells a jester's tale,
While daisies giggle without fail.

Bees play tag across the sun's ray,
Buzzing jokes in their busy ballet.
A sunflower yawns, stretching its face,
While roses spin in a fragrant race.

Pansies ponder with grinning delight,
Joking about who blooms best at night.
Leaves rustle in fitful glee,
As the breeze joins in, light and free.

Reflections dance in petals bright,
You never know who's in your sight.
Plant a smile, let the laughter spread,
In this garden where whimsy's bred.

Quietude of the Untouched

In a garden where oddities grow,
Laughter bubbles, seeds in tow.
A gnome in the corner does a jig,
While carrots plot to dance a big.

Butterflies laugh at the snail's slow pace,
Mice throw parties, a wild embrace.
The sun beams down, a warmth so bright,
Chasing clouds that give a fright.

Dandelions giggle as they flow,
The breeze gives them a playful throw.
A toad croaks out a silly tune,
Making frogs hop under the moon.

In this patch, the chaos is sweet,
With mischief woven in every beat.
Join the fun in this green parade,
Where silly moments never fade.

Murmurs from the Meadow

In the meadow where giggles grow,
Bumblebees wear hats, don't you know?
Grass blades tickle, pushing apart,
A patchwork quilt for laughter's art.

The daisies gossip, gossip galore,
While butterflies flit and explore.
'Did you see that leap and sway?'
'Oh yes! They danced the whole day!'

A rabbit hops, giving a wink,
While daisies whisper, 'Let's make a drink!'
With every sway, there's chaos and cheer,
In this meadow, joy's always near.

So come and join the merriment loud,
Nature's jesters are sure to wow.
For here in green, life's one big jest,
In whispers of fun, we find our best.

The Language of the Earth

Beneath the soil, a chatter fest,
Roots gossiping is quite the quest.
'Did you hear what the worm said?'
'Oh yes, the juiciest, 'bout a bed!'

The rocks chime in, all rough and tough,
'Pick a side, this game's quite rough!'
While mushrooms giggle, holding court,
With tiny caps, making bids for sport.

In the sunshine, the daisies chime,
'Let's have a laugh, it's blooming time!'
And every breeze carries whispers loud,
Echoing joy to nature's crowd.

So listen close, don't miss the cue,
For playful banter is meant for you.
Earth speaks softly but with a grin,
A comedy show you can't miss, join in!

Shadows Among the Leaves

In twilight's glow, shadows creep,
With giggles, the bushes leap.
A squirrel whispers, 'Yo, I'm here!'
While a bug plays the tambourine near.

The owls hoot a joke or two,
As fireflies bring a glowing crew.
Even the flowers join the jest,
With petals that sparkle, they're the best!

A cat prances, claiming high ground,
While the daisies twirl all around.
They share tales of the nightime spree,
'Oh, the things we've seen!' they decree.

Through laughter and rustle, the night takes flight,
Where shadows dance and spirits unite.
So wander forth and join the fun,
Among the leaves, joy's never done.

Tales of the Untamed

In the garden, secrets sway,
With greens that laugh and play.
A leaf with legs, it skips around,
Singing tunes without a sound.

A dandelion in a hat,
Claims to be the king of brat.
While clovers dance in pairs so bold,
They tell tales of the wild and old.

The thistles throw a wild tea,
'Join our party, come and see!'
With every breeze, a giggle shared,
Nature's humor, never spared.

In this realm, no frown can last,
Where even roots have stories cast.
So if you wander, heed the call,
For laughter reigns, and joy stands tall.

Sighs of the Sprouting Sky

Up above, the clouds give a wink,
As seeds sprout tales no one could think.
With giggles of raindrops, they spring from the ground,
Among the bright flowers, pure joy can be found.

The daisies conspire, while clovers play tricks,
Telling stories of earthy old flicks.
The sun gives a grin, lighting up the scene,
As laughter is spun where the grass grows green.

A grasshopper strums on a twig like a loot,
While ants move around in a jubilant suit.
The wind carries chuckles, a symphony fine,
As nature's hilarious rhythms align.

So let's tip our hats to the sprouting sky,
Where every breath draws forth a new high.
In this garden of giggles, where fun never ends,
We learn from the earth, our whimsical friends.

Legends of the Leafy Realm

In a land where the green crowns sway,
Tall tales are spun at the end of the day.
With a chuckle and cheer, they wrap around,
As mischievous tales start to abound.

The mushrooms giggle, the toadstools sing,
From tiny sprouts, endless stories spring.
A magical tree with a twisty trunk,
Cradles the laughter of every zany punk.

Frogs in tuxedos throw a grand feast,
While butterflies waltz, they never cease.
The critters gather, a party so bright,
Under the moon, they dance with delight.

So here's to the moments, the legends unfold,
In the leafy realm, where hilarity's gold.
With whispers and chuckles, we join in the fun,
A celebration of life when the day is done.

The Aroma of Hidden Truths

In a garden where secrets grow,
The flowers giggle with a playful glow.
A breeze carries tales of silly dreams,
While sunlight dances in sparkling beams.

Bees buzz around with a cheeky rhyme,
Gathering nectar, saving us time.
A squirrel drags a half-eaten snack,
Whispers of munchies, no looking back.

Laughter erupts from the patchy grass,
As rabbits hold court, they sip from a glass.
Innocent laughter fills the warm air,
A world of wonder, a lively affair.

So join the fest with a smirk and a grin,
For in this garden, we all wear a pin.
A sweet little token of joy and of cheer,
Where every scent brings the friends we hold dear.

Intimate Chants of the Earth

In the soil, chuckles blend,
Worms and bugs, they softly send.
Grassy knolls roll in merry cheer,
With every blade, they mock the year.

Pebbles giggle as they lie,
In the stream where echoes sigh.
Mountains chuckle with a grin,
As clouds parade, it's time to spin.

Mossy patches plot their schemes,
Crickets dream up silly themes.
With every root that gently sways,
Earth's humor brightens all our days.

Whispers tickle, laughter grows,
In this place where friendship flows.
A world alive with playful heart,
Nature's witticisms impart.

Murmurs in the Jungle Shadows

Monkeys grinning, swinging high,
Jungle tales as birds fly by.
Leaves rustle, whispering fun,
As sunlight breaks, the day's begun.

Geckos chat on rocks so warm,
Their quirky banter, quite the charm.
Vines twist with a cheeky flair,
Tickling noses with fresh air.

Tigers grin in shady spots,
Under trees with playful knots.
Every rustle, a jest unfolds,
In the canopy, laughter rolls.

Through the shadows, giggles burst,
In this wild, we'll never thirst.
The jungle hums a lively tune,
Nature's jesters, night and noon.

Silent Stories of the Wild

Squirrels whisper off the trees,
Flipping tails in breezy tease.
A badger smirks from beneath the ground,
With cheeky tales that know no sound.

The owls hoot in droll surprise,
As rabbits plot their big disguise.
Every bush holds a grin so sly,
While crickets chirp their own high pie.

A sloth shrugs, quite content,
In a slow-motion jest, it's spent.
Butterflies flit in patterned pride,
While the daisies share what they've tried.

Amidst the shade, secrets play,
Nature's humor, come what may.
In silent woods, the laughter stirs,
As every creature gently purrs.

The Lush Language of Nature

In the garden, jokes grow tall,
Chortles hidden by the wall.
Leaves gossip on a sunny day,
Tickling toes in a playful way.

Ladybugs with wiggly dance,
Share secrets in a merry trance.
Sunflowers laugh, they nod their heads,
Sharing tales as daylight spreads.

Breezes bring a teasing song,
Nature laughs where we belong.
Roots entwined in silly binds,
Chuckle lightly, oh how it shines!

Take a stroll, let laughter ring,
In the greenery, joy takes wing.
Nature's tongue speaks tongue-in-cheek,
In every nook, there's fun to seek.

The Lullaby of Leaves

The leaves conspire on the breeze,
Telling tales with cheeky ease.
A gnome peeks from a hollow tree,
Winking at you. Can't you see?

Cracks in bark, a smirking face,
Nature's humor shows its grace.
Roots wiggle, planting jokes anew,
While daisies blush in morning dew.

A sleepy snail dreams of grand things,
Like races with the bees on wings.
Pinecones ponder, should we play?
While shadows dance in bright ballet.

Giggles echo through the glade,
In this laughter, we've all stayed.
Remember, nature loves to tease,
So come and join, let laugh with ease!

Nature's Murmurs

Underneath the canopy,
Frogs exchange a symphony.
Caterpillars sport a tie,
At the gala of the sky.

Crickets chirp a dandy tune,
In the light of the big moon.
Fireflies join in the jest,
A flickering little fest!

The river grins as it flows fast,
Tickling stones, oh what a blast!
A floating leaf rides like a king,
While reeds sway and sweetly sing.

Listen close, you'll hear the song,
Nature's humor, all along.
Bursting laughter in the breeze,
Join the fun, that's sure to please!

Tender Communications

Petals chat in colors bright,
Just like kids, all pure delight.
Butterflies in tight-knit swirls,
Share their dreams with all the girls.

Bees be-bumble in the sun,
Telling jokes, oh what fun!
Hummingbirds with tiny grins,
Sip sweet nectar, start again!

Clouds drift by with silly pouts,
Making shapes, oh what it's about!
Sunny rays are in on the gag,
Chasing shadows, wave the flag!

Winds will giggle, softly sway,
Tickling leaves in the ballet.
Nature whispers all around,
In this dance, joy's profound!

Enigmas of the Woods

In the woods, a rustle's cheer,
Squirrels giggle, oh so near.
Mossy rocks have secrets, too,
Whispered secrets, just for you.

Foxes prance with mischief bright,
Chasing shadows, what a sight!
Underneath the mushroom cap,
Lies a sleepy, cozy nap.

Branches sway in silly dance,
Leaves are laughing, take a chance!
Nature's jesters, wild and free,
Join the frolic, come and see!

The woods are filled with quirky tales,
Of owls wearing tiny veils.
A wiggly worm does a jig,
So join the fun, it's quite big!

Profound Silence of the Thicket

Amidst the thorns, silence reigns,
Yet the laughter softly feigns.
A wise old owl cracks a joke,
While underfoot a dandelion spoke!

Under the cover, shadows dip,
In secret games, they laugh and skip.
A modest fern plays peek-a-boo,
With an insect squad that's passing through.

The stillness hides a vibrant mirth,
As creatures plot a little birth.
Of whimsical joy, a sprightly band,
In a world that's simply unplanned.

In the hush, a twinkle glows,
As evening drops and starlight flows.
The thicket holds its playful charm,
Protecting laughter, keeping warm.

Enchanted Portrayals of Green

Nature paints with vibrant hues,
A canvas where absurdity brews.
The grass giggles as we stroll,
With antics that could take a toll!

Petals blush with teasing grace,
As bees engage in a dizzy race.
A flower checks its leafy hat,
And says, "You look like quite a brat!"

The mushrooms act as silly jesters,
While crickets play like concert testers.
Each creature wears a playful guise,
With mischief sparkling in their eyes.

They spin and twirl, a lively clan,
In this enchanted, green-filled land.
Where laughter seeds the fertile ground,
And joy, in every shade is found.

Calm Under the Canopy

Beneath the leaves, a giggle grows,
As critters play in funny rows.
A squirrel juggles acorns bold,
While dreaming of tales yet untold.

The sun peeks through with cheeky glee,
Tickling the ground from a leafy tree.
Dandelions boast their sunny smiles,
As rabbits hop in silly styles.

A lazy breeze collects the sounds,
Of bubbling laughter all around.
Beneath the arch of emerald green,
Every moment feels like a dream.

With whimsy swirling 'round like mist,
Nature's joy cannot be missed.
As shadows dance upon the ground,
In this sanctuary, fun is found.

The Swaying Symphony

In the breeze, the green folks sway,
Dancing wildly, come what may.
Each blade hums a quirky tale,
But beware, they might inhale!

Laughter ripples through the field,
As secrets of the soil are revealed.
With every giggle, roots entwine,
Making jokes over dinner wine.

A joyful tune from nature's band,
Playing tunes we can't quite understand.
They throw a party, wild and free,
Inviting all the bugs, you see!

In the twilight, shadows cast,
The plants whisper of a time long past.
Their leafy chatter, light as air,
Makes you wonder if they care.

Veiled Melodies of the Garden

In corners lush and hideaway,
Melodies twirl and frolic, they sway,
Plants share secrets, come what may,
While sunflowers grin at their ballet.

The marigolds hum a cheery tune,
As fireflies dance beneath the moon,
Frogs don tuxedos, all in swoon,
A serenade makes the critters croon.

With petals as props, they put on shows,
A silly waltz by the cheeky crows,
Their feathery friends join in with their bows,
Laughter erupts from the stemmed rows.

The roses giggle, a fragrant delight,
As nighttime brings a whimsical sight,
In this garden of glee, pure delight,
Where melodies echo, the heart takes flight.

The Silent Language of the Grass

Amidst the blades, a chatter grows,
A riot of whispers; no one knows,
What antics lie in the grass's prose,
As giggles echo, and laughter flows.

The daisies gossip, tipsy and light,
About the ants that dance at night,
With crickets chirping, a comical sight,
As moonlight spills, all feels just right.

Each breeze carries a playful shout,
Gusts that swirl, spinning dreams about,
In this grassy realm, beyond all doubt,
Nature's jesters are parading out.

Tiny creatures strut with flair,
The shyest beetle jumps in the air,
Making jokes no one can declare,
In this symphony, no need to care.

Whispers Amidst the Ferns

In a patch of green where giggles bloom,
Ferns hold secrets, dispelling gloom,
Mice don tiny hats, ready to zoom,
As nature hums a merry tune.

Crickets pulse with a winking grin,
Twirling around like they're on spin,
Little parties where friends all win,
With bouquets of laughter tucked within.

Owls wink knowingly from their perch,
As hedgehogs host a wobbly search,
In this jolly, woodland, wondrous church,
Foliage flutters, ready to lurch.

Bumblebees join in the merry dance,
Whizzing in circles, a comical trance,
Leaves chuckle softly, a leafy romance,
As twinkling stars invite a chance.

A Shimmering Undercurrent of Sound

In the garden where giggles play,
A bubble of laughter floats away,
With leaves that dance, they tease and sway,
As squirrels join in, on their display.

Bees are tapping on secret doors,
A choir of critters, the sweet encore,
Chirping tunes on the forest floor,
While butterflies show off, wanting more.

The whispers weave through the tall grass,
Silly secrets none can surpass,
Even the daisies sway and sass,
As laughter rings; what a joyous mass!

When twilight comes, the frogs take part,
With ribbit-rap that's off the chart,
In the frolic 'neath the starlit art,
Each note a giggle, a pulsing heart.

Unraveled in the Underbrush

In the underbrush, a story brews,
Of cheeky critters and playful news,
Snakes play dice, the toads all cheer,
In this wild mess, nothing's unclear.

Ferns flap their leaves in curious joy,
While beetles parry, the cute decoy,
A hedgehog chuckles, all spines in sync,
In tangled greens, they laugh and wink.

Mice host parties on a crumbly pile,
Finding fun in the wild style,
As shadows dance on the forest floor,
Laughter echoes, and spirits soar.

So wander low where mischief blooms,
And join the chatter 'neath leafy rooms,
For in each twist, you'll find the bliss,
In the underbrush, we laugh amiss!

Harmonies of the Herbal

In fields where green and giggles grow,
Herbs conspire with the winds that blow,
Mint tells tales of the freshest drinks,
While basil laughs and softly winks.

Thyme stretches out with a playful yawn,
Sage sings songs from dusk till dawn,
In the herbal choir, all find their tune,
Creating laughter 'neath the moon.

Parsley joins with a cheeky shout,
In playful banter, they twist about,
With every breeze, a joke is told,
In the midst of green, laughter unfolds.

So sway to the rhythm, let humor flow,
In the herbal realm, let the laughter grow,
For every sprig has a story to weave,
In nature's tale, we all believe.

Petals Speak Softly

Petals whisper tales in bloom,
Of sunshine days and garden gloom,
In colors bright, each vibrant joke,
They giggle softly, never choke.

A daisy winks, a rose does cheer,
'Why are we here?' it asks the deer,
The tulips blush, 'Just for the fun!'
As bees take flight, their pollens run.

Every sprout holds a secret grin,
Telling stories of where they've been,
In the garden, no need to rush,
Nature plays, inspires the hush.

In this realm, where laughter sings,
Petals flaunt their joyful wings,
So stop and laugh, grab a seat,
Nature's humor can't be beat!

Messages on the Breeze

Leaves chuckle as they dance,
Breezes carry jokes askance,
Nature's whispers, sly and spry,
And all the flowers wink and sigh.

A dandelion giggles bright,
While crickets laugh into the night,
The grass blades nod with cheeky glee,
Gossiping in harmony, you see!

Squirrels comment, tails in tow,
As rabbits enter the comedy show,
With every rustle, a punchline grows,
In nature's realm, laughter flows.

So heed the rustles in the air,
For jokes are blooming everywhere,
The vines twist in a playful tease,
And chuckle softly with the breeze.

Nature's Soft Secrets

Among the petals, secrets bloom,
Where petals wiggle, chasing gloom.
The bees gossip with a joyful hum,
As flowers share tales, oh so glum.

The wind plays tricks with each green frond,
Tickling the leaves, they ripple, respond.
Nature's laughter, soft and sweet,
Echoes in the roots and on the street.

Even the rain has a quirky way,
Of drumming rhythms come out to play.
As puddles giggle underfoot,
Each ripple leaps like a little foot.

So when you wander through this land,
Hear the chuckles and understand.
Nature's soft secrets, joyful, alive,
In every bud, humor will thrive.

Whispers of Nature's Hidden Realm

In shadows where the critters play,
Nature's whispers come into sway.
The toads croak out a cheeky tune,
While squirrels plot beneath the moon.

Beneath the ferns, a fox eavesdrops,
On the cackle of giggling crops.
Even mushrooms have a tale,
Of how they danced in night's pale veil.

Beetles boast of journeys wide,
As ladybugs just laugh and slide.
In this realm of wild jest,
Each plant and critter knows the best.

With rustling leaves as their delight,
They sprinkle humor through the night.
In the whispers, joy's unfurled,
A funny show within their world.

The Quiet Soliloquy of Seeds

Tiny seeds in silent plots,
Whisper dreams of gardens hot.
They chuckle at the surface's plight,
Rooting for a higher height.

From a pot, a bean hops high,
Pretending it's a bird in the sky.
Peas play hide-and-seek with ants,
While sunflower seeds practice their dance.

In dormancy, they share some puns,
About the rain and burning suns.
Each a player in nature's game,
These tiny jesters seek their fame.

As they sprout from earth's embrace,
They throw their jokes with leafy grace.
In this quiet, growth-filled spree,
Seeds laugh together, wild and free.

Leafy Confessions of the Earth

In the garden, leaves conspire,
Sharing secrets of their fire.
Each rustle hides a joke or two,
Beneath the sun, they giggle new.

Roots are plotting, oh so sly,
Telling tales as time slips by.
A dandelion snickers in the breeze,
Winking at the bumblebees.

The daisies dance in playful cheer,
While the broccoli cracks jokes, loud and clear.
Nature's laughter fills the air,
As flowers tease without a care.

So let us join this leafy fun,
Where every sprout feels like a pun.
In this patch, we find delight,
As plants concoct their funny sight.

Hidden Melodies of Nature

In the hush of the grove, laughter creeps,
As whispers of grass cut through the deeps.
Frogs croon softly to the rhythm of night,
While fireflies twinkle, igniting delight.

The rustle of leaves is a comical tune,
Played by the wind in the hush of the moon.
Bunnies in tuxedos hop to the beat,
While night-blooming flowers are dressed up neat.

As owls hoot riddles in a comedic tone,
Even the moths start to buzz and moan.
Nature's a stage filled with quirky plays,
Where each giggle and snicker always stays.

So lift your spirits, join in the cheer,
For the playful serenade of nature is near.
In each vibrant corner, find giggles and glee,
With hidden melodies, let your heart be free!

The Dance of Sundrenched Serenity

Under the sun, the daffodils sway,
While lazy clouds play hide and seek all day.
A squirrel, with flair, steals the show,
Twisting and turning, stealing the glow.

Grass tickles toes in a wild parade,
While shadows dance; they can't be swayed.
A ladybug winks, "Let's break some rules!"
As playful breezes scatter the pools.

The sunbeams giggle, lighting a path,
Through fields of joy and celestial math.
Launching daisies into a spin,
In this silly ballet, we all win!

So let's dance lightly, free as the breeze,
In the sundrenched magic, we find our ease.
With each little laugh, let's cheer for today,
In the delightful moments, let's forever stay!

Fragrant Whims of the Wild

A bug in shades sips nectar divine,
Flower petals giggle, 'It's party time!'
The wind tells tales of a dapper snail,
Who glides with swagger on a leafy trail.

Crickets choir with a tune so neat,
While ants form lines, quick on their feet.
A butterfly flutters, fancy and free,
As if to say, 'Come dance with me!'

The scents entwine in a breezy chuckle,
While mushrooms giggle beneath their shuffle.
Carnivorous plants with a grinning glint,
Offer a bite—just a little hint!

So let us prance through the fragrant glade,
Where joy and laughter will never fade.
In the wild's embrace, we find our cheer,
Join the whimsy, the fun is near!

The Spirit of Verdancy

In a patch where the green things grow,
Lurking critters put on a show.
Dandelions giggle, grasshoppers hum,
While a lazy cat ponders, 'Where's my crumb?'

Bees in bow ties with wings of flair,
Finding nectar; they've got the air!
Mossy carpets on which to prance,
Twirling leaves in a joyous dance.

Nature's laughter in every breeze,
Whispers secrets from leafy trees.
A frog croaks jokes, the sun gives a wink,
Life's a party, don't you think?

So let's raise a toast to the sprout,
Where the silly and sprightly dance about.
In a world that's bright and absurdly grand,
Join the fun in this verdant land!

Voices of the Overgrowth

In the overgrowth, jokes abound,
Every vine a comic sound,
Caterpillars tell tall tales,
While crickets strum with wiggly wails.

Branches sway in silent glee,
Nature's laughter, wild and free,
Spiderwebs craft punchlines meek,
As squirrels scamper, play hide and seek.

Roots entwined in playful brawl,
Every leaf a call to all,
In the chaos, joy unfurls,
The overgrowth, where laughter twirls.

A medley of the greenest fun,
In every shade, a secret pun.

Harmony in the Haze

In the haze, giggles soar,
Clouds spin tales we can't ignore,
Laughter drips from drifty air,
Each breath brings a secret flair.

Shadows wiggle, colors fade,
Nature's antics never weighed,
Through the fog, a jest is seen,
Life's a stage on which we beam.

Mushrooms peek with cheeky grins,
Puffballs puff with silly spins,
A chorus of the quirkiest cheer,
In this haze, the fun is clear.

Harmony rides on the breeze,
Joyfully wrapped in leafy tease.

The Serenity of Flora

Petals bloom with mischief bright,
Sunbeams tickle, feeling right,
Bees buzz tunes of silly dance,
Each flower wears a playful glance.

Ferns sway like they know a joke,
With a wink, they gently poke,
Breezes carry giggles clear,
Every leaf, a comrade dear.

Mossy rocks in quiet jest,
Whisper tales of nature's best,
In this green and lovely place,
Laughter lingers, leaves embrace.

From the roots to blooms up high,
Flora's harmony will never die.

Secrets of the Wild

In the wild, secrets spin,
Little leaves chuckle loud,
Bugs play cards on the skin,
Roots dance, in laughter proud.

Twisting vines, whispers fly,
Buds giggle, can't be shy,
Nature's jesters in the sun,
Every joke, a little pun.

Frogs croak like old-time jesters,
Mice prance in sneaky pacts,
Swaying grass in wild gestures,
Life here, full of funny acts.

Nature's punsters hold their ground,
With every rustle, joy is found.

Nature's Murmurs and Silent Reveries

Through the woods, where whispers play,
Nature's secrets dance and sway.
A rustling leaf, a gust of air,
Sprouts chuckle at our silly stare.

The mushrooms giggle, sprouting tall,
While insects hold a rambunctious ball.
Old oaks grumble, branches sway,
In nature's hands, we all find a way.

A chipmunk's nibble, a quick retreat,
While flowers cringe in laughter sweet.
The squirrels plot with acorn hats,
Creating tales with all their spats.

So listen close to the verdant glee,
Join the frolic, just wait and see.
For in this realm of gentle grace,
Funny whispers find their place.

Whimsy of the Wandering Vines

Vines that twist and twirl about,
Share tall tales with a playful shout.
They wriggle, giggle, in the breeze,
Plotting mischief with such ease.

The creeping things, with best of friends,
Make up rules, but never ends.
Corn cobs chuckle, carrots grieve,
As the garden weaves and schemes to cleave.

A snicker erupts from leafy beds,
As gossip spreads among their heads.
The wayward sprouts play peek-a-boo,
In this green world, anything's true.

So stroll along the tangled trail,
Where every vine is sure to sail.
With laughter woven in their lines,
Discover joy in these lonesome vines.

Soft Speeches in the Sunlight

Basking bugs in sunlit bliss,
Share tales with smiles you can't dismiss.
A dandelion, bold and bright,
Claims the day with sheer delight.

Sunflowers sway, with heads held high,
Whispering secrets, oh my, oh my!
The bees buzz softly, taking notes,
Claiming stories from every throats.

A squirrel laughs, a raccoon laughs,
While ivy climbs and plays at gaffes.
Nature's laughter, a joyful sound,
In sunlight's grasp, the world's unbound.

So if you wander, take a pause,
Join the chatter, give applause.
For in the bright and rosy glade,
Funny tales in sunshine laid.

The Unseen Chorus of Flora

In the garden, gossip blooms,
Laughter dances, shatters glooms.
Petals giggle, roots conspire,
To weave a tale that lifts us higher.

Beneath the leaves, a secret crew,
Plants conspire, all just for you.
The daisies tease the sleepy bees,
While tulips tango with the breeze.

Swaying stems with silly prance,
Entwine in nature's crazy dance.
A frog jumps in, the crowd goes wild,
As blooms break free, nature's child.

So next time you walk through the green,
Listen close to what's unseen.
The plants may plot or spin a yarn,
With each twist, a timeless charm.

Subdued Reverberations

In dappled woods, the shadows collide,
Where a snail auditions for slowest slide.
A raccoon dabbles in gourmet finds,
Collecting rare snacks that tickle the minds.

Low whispers are heard—murmurs and chortles,
As foxes sneak snacks from the nearby portals.
"Did you see that?" the gopher proclaims,
"Last week, I duped them with my trench coat games!"

Echoes of laughter float through the trees,
As chipmunks concoct new zany strategies.
The world feels alive with delightful pranks,
Even a log joins in, full of deep thanks.

So wander through echoes of nature's own cheer,
Where every soft chuckle is music to hear.
Under the subtle, suspenseful display,
Humor unfolds in a whimsical way.

Threads of Nature's Tapestry

Each blossom unfurls with a giggle and grin,
As ants run the runway, their march is akin.
Butterflies flutter, in silk they dress,
Posing like models, no need to impress.

The sun beamed bright; on flowers they prance,
While bees throw a party, inviting the chance.
"I'll be DJ," buzzed the loud, silly fellow,
As they dance to the rhythm, so bright and yellow.

The wind whispers tales through the swaying grass,
Tickly and playful, it's happy to pass.
It steals hats from heads and then plays coy hide-and-seek,
Leaving behind laughter that echoes unique.

So here in the garden, fabric of fun,
Nature weaves stories under the sun.
Every thread spun with giggles galore,
A tapestry vibrant, who could ask for more?

The Essence of Stillness

In the quiet, a frog croaks a tune,
On lily pads basking, under the moon.
A turtle, quite slow, wears a bow tie,
As dragonflies laugh, passing by with a sigh.

Pond reflections, a mirror of cheer,
Where goldfish tell tales only they can hear.
A heron poses; it thinks it's a model,
While the reeds roll their eyes, in the throttle.

The sun sets softly, evening takes stage,
Crickets pin stories on nature's own page.
A nocturnal orchestra, wild and free,
Playing the score of pure melody.

In this canvas of calm, laughter persists,
With each rustle of leaves, nature insists.
For moments of stillness aren't quiet in vain,
They're the jesters that twirl on the edge of the plain.

Reflections of the Wild

In a forest where giggles grow,
Squirrels debate the best hide-and-seek show.
Mice wear hats, quite a sight to see,
Dancing on mushrooms with utmost glee.

The trees gossip in rustling tones,
As raccoons play chess with sticks and stones.
A rabbit judges, keen in its stare,
While owls hoot jokes into cool night air.

Beneath the moon's watchful, winking eye,
Crickets recite poetry with a sigh.
Fireflies flash, like laughter in a jar,
Whispering secrets from near and far.

Nature's a comedian in vibrant attire,
Each creature a performer, hearts afire.
So come and partake in this woodland spree,
Where joy dances free like a leaf in the breeze.

Conversations with the Ferns

The ferns are having a jolly chat,
Discussing the tales of a wandering cat.
With fronds held high and gleaming green,
They gossip louder than you'd have seen.

One fern tells of a sunbeam's plight,
Who lost its way just to feel bright.
Huddling together, they start to sway,
While sharing secrets from yesterday.

A snail, intrigued, slides on by,
Listening in with a curious eye.
As laughter ripples through the glen,
The ferns embrace their joyous zen.

Among the roots and twinkling leaves,
You'll find their chuckles and playful heaves.
In every curve and every bend,
Nature's humor has no end.

Nature's Quiet Complaints

The trees are tired of all the talk,
Of squirrels stealing their hard-earned stock.
They sigh and sway, a leafy groan,
While ants march on, no sense of tone.

A flower claims it needs a break,
"I'm not a cake for bugs to stake!"
Yet bees ignore the protest cries,
Dancing around like clever spies.

The raindrops chuckle, fall with grace,
Tickling leaves in this wild place.
"Stay grounded, roots!" they cheekily tease,
As puddles form with whimsical ease.

So listen close to nature's grumble,
In quiet corners, you might stumble.
For every complaint hides a wink,
A fun-filled world makes us think.

Subtle Echoes of the Past

In the garden where time elopes,
The daisies weave some daring hopes.
A gnome with a crooked little hat,
Sits pondering his own old cat.

There's gossip among the tulips bright,
Sharing tales of a wild flight.
A beetle brags of worldly charms,
While avoiding the flower's arms.

The sunbeams stretch, they start to tease,
As shadows skedaddle with the breeze.
They whisper 'bout the days gone by,
While birds roll 'round and laugh up high.

So pause and hear the echoes call,
In every petal, there's a fall.
The past may giggle, the present, cheer,
In this funny world, we hold dear.

The Lullaby of Lost Shadows

In a park where shadows dance,
A squirrel holds a secret glance.
With acorns stacked and nuts to spare,
He sings to leaves without a care.

The sunlight flickers, plays its game,
A butterfly thinks it's the same.
Chasing whispers, all aflight,
They giggle under fading light.

A dandelion with dreams so grand,
Wants to be part of a rock band.
It strums its seeds, a breezy tune,
While ants march off to join the moon.

So when you walk and hear that jest,
Just know the grass is at its best.
With every chuckle from the ground,
A funny story can be found.

The Soft Heartbeat of the Wild

In the meadow, a quail makes a scene,
Flapping around, like a well-cooked bean.
Grasshoppers leap, with a jovial spray,
Tickling the daisies in a merry ballet.

Beneath a green blanket, a turtle's slow crawl,
Smiling around, he won't hurry at all.
Sunflowers chuckle, heads swaying in cheer,
While laughter rustles through the foliage near.

Lurking Notes of the Undergrowth

In the thicket, a frog leaps with a croak,
Tickling the daisies, a humorous joke.
Snakes glide past, with a sly little grin,
As the wind carries tales of where they've been.

A playful mole digs, his plans askew,
Dreaming of treasures, but where is his view?
The hedgehog giggles, she knows all the tricks,
While ants march by, lost in their mix.

Twilight Whispers of the Greenery

Stars above peek, eyes twinkling with glee,
Watching the raccoons hold their grand spree.
Moonlight drapes over the sleepy old trees,
As crickets chuckle, swaying with ease.

A fox tells secrets to the night air,
With all of nature performing its flair.
Owl joins in, a wise old toad's shout,
Echoes of laughter, no room for doubt.

Serene Echoes Amongst the Foliage

In the garden, a squirrel does dance,
Trying to steal a brave rabbit's chance.
The flowers gossip in colors so bright,
While the sun giggles, just out of sight.

Bees buzz by with a playful hum,
Chasing each other, oh what a fun!
Butterflies flirt with the petals up high,
As leaves wink softly and flutter to fly.

Nature's Delicate Dialogues

In sunny spots, whispers collide,
Daisies chat, no need to hide.
Squirrels pause for a fruity laugh,
While dandelions wave in the path.

Chirps of birds in a playful tone,
Echo the joys of seeds they've sown.
With frolic and fun, they greet the day,
In nature's room where giggles stay.

The Pulse Beneath the Soil

Beneath the earth, a raucous jest,
A ticklish root, the soil's best guest.
Worms are the comedians of the bunch,
They wriggle and squirm, never out to lunch.

The drumming sound of busy ants,
Tap with glee in their tiny pants.
A dance of life, a vibrant show,
Underground parties where no one knows.

Hushed Revelations

In corners dark, the shadows play,
Plants conspire in a leafy ballet.
Voices low, they always share,
Of sunlit jaunts and fragrant air.

A pair of paws tiptoe near,
Flowers giggle, knowing no fear.
Buds unfold with a grin wide,
As mystery blooms with nature's pride.

In the Soft Embrace of Silence

In the garden, secrets sway,
Leaves giggle at the end of day.
Roots beneath, they plot and scheme,
While gardeners chase an elusive dream.

Petals whisper tales so bright,
Of moonlit dances in the night.
Every breeze, a ticklish tease,
Nature's laughter, sure to please.

The Unspoken Rhythm of the Glade

In the glade, a heartbeat's pulse,
Leaves perform their leafy waltz.
Twigs and vines join up the dance,
Every rustle, a chance romance.

Frogs composing cheeky tunes,
Next to playful firefly moons.
"Hop along!" the toads all call,
Nature's merriment invites us all.

A squirrel juggling acorn snacks,
Laughter echoing, no heart lacks.
Swinging low, the branches sway,
Join the mischief, come what may.

With every dawn, the story spins,
Rotating jokes as daylight begins.
In the glade, what joy unfurls,
Nature's jokes, a world of swirls.

Night's Gentle Warnings from the Fields

When the stars begin to wink,
Crickets start their playful sync.
Mice in hats, a silent cheer,
Whispers echo, "Night is near!"

Moonlight dances on dewy leaves,
Gentle truths the twilight weaves.
"Don't be silly, roots don't bark,
But boy, they sure can leave a mark!"

Fields are buzzing with delight,
Each shadow holds a jest tonight.
"Watch your step, the daisies might,
Sprout a giggle in the moonlight!"

Under cover of the night,
Nature's humor takes to flight.
Laughing crops that sway and sway,
Join the fun, night's here to play.

When the Flora Sings Low

When the bushes start to hum,
Bumblebees get up and drum.
Every petal sways with grace,
Having fun, no need for space.

With a wink, the grass agrees,
Let's play hide and seek with breeze.
Every stalk a hidden grin,
Ticklish winds, let games begin.

Low voices barely reach the air,
Cactus pricks a little dare.
"Who's the funniest?" a leaf will ask,
"Come on friends, let's wear a mask!"

In the glade, they come alive,
Nature's laughter, simple thrive.
So, if you listen, you might find,
Flora sings with a cheeky mind.

Echoing Secrets of the Roots

Underneath the soil's gray cloak,
Giggles rise from roots that poke.
Tiny whispers, secrets shared,
Even the bugs can't help but stare.

Dancing shadows in the sun,
Every leaf a joke, a pun.
Laughter sprouting, wild and free,
Nature's charm, a jubilee.

Beneath the moon's mischievous grin,
Silly sprites begin to spin.
Tap your toes to the earth's own tune,
Join the ruckus 'neath the moon.

So lend an ear to nature's glee,
In every seed, a chuckle's key.
Let the roots tickle your funny bone,
In this garden, you're never alone.

Secrets Carried by the Breeze

Carried away on a playful breeze,
Grasshoppers leap with enviable ease.
'Who's the best jumper?' they challenge in fun,
While dandelions puff, 'We've only just begun!'

The wind whispers tales of the flowers so bold,
With petals that shimmer in colors untold.
A rabbit joins in, with a cheeky grin,
'In this frolicsome field, let's all spin!'

Echoes of the Hidden Grove

In the hidden grove where giggles arise,
A raccoon spins tales beneath the skies.
'Did you see that squirrel with acorn in tow?'
Laughter erupts, 'The joke's on that show!'

The shadows hum tunes of ridiculous glee,
With fireflies twinkling, oh what a spree!
A butterfly flutters, 'Join my parade!'
As the trees snicker, 'We're never afraid.'

Whispers from the Verdant Depths

Beneath the ferns, secrets unfold,
With mushrooms plotting, or so I've been told.
A centipede struts in a patterned spree,
'Who can outshine my fancy shoes spree?'

Gossip flows like a bubbling brook,
With ivy entwined in a lively nook.
The bumblebees chuckle, pollinate with pride,
While laughing leaves sway side to side.

Subtle Voices in the Thicket

In the thicket where shadows prance,
The leaves giggle, oh what a chance!
Squirrels debate, with a comical flair,
'Who's the sassiest creature in this wild lair?'

Breezy whispers tease the tall grass,
The daisies dance, never a dull pass.
A frog croaks loudly, 'I'm the real king!'
While crickets join in for a lighthearted sing.

Twilight Murmurs

As night descends with a velvet cloak,
The plants gather round for a joke or a poke.
One vine drapes low and whispers a pun,
While crickets join in their evening fun.

The petals giggle as stars ignite,
With stories of dewdrops glimmering bright.
In twilight's embrace, they share with glee,
The joy of being wild and free!

Enigmatic Brushstrokes of Life

A painter bee splashes color on blooms,
While ants waltz in their tiny costumes.
Each petal whispers a mischievous plot,
To keep the garden in a playful spot.

A dandelion dressed in dapper gold,
Claims it once had a story quite bold.
With laughter and pollen, they all conspire,
Creating humor in nature's attire.

The Gentle Ties of Nature

A daisy once tried to hug a rose,
But found out thorns are not friends, it knows.
Their laughter rings clear as raindrops fall,
Nature's own comedy, loved by all.

The trees share stories in rustling tones,
About squirrels who've lost all their phones.
Grins emerge on branches high and low,
As they swap tales of the winds that blow.

Secret Lives of Leaves

In a garden where gossip grows,
Leaves exchange secrets, goodness knows.
One claims to have danced with the breeze,
While another insists it sways with ease.

A leaf with a hat, so chic and bright,
Boasts of a party that lasted all night.
They chuckle as shadows creep and play,
Plotting mischief by the light of day.

Original title:
Weed Whispers

Copyright © 2025 Creative Arts Management OÜ
All rights reserved.

Author: Gabriel Kingsley
ISBN HARDBACK: 978-1-80566-599-1
ISBN PAPERBACK: 978-1-80566-884-8